STAR-CROSSED LOVE

star-crossed love

Courtney Gorter

UNION
SQUARE
& CO.

NEW YORK

**UNION
SQUARE
& CO.**

NEW YORK

UNION SQUARE & CO. and the distinctive
Union Square & Co. logo are trademarks of Sterling
Publishing Co., Inc.

Union Square & Co., LLC, is a subsidiary of Sterling Publishing Co., Inc.

ISBN 978-1-4549-4620-5
ISBN 978-1-4549-4621-2 (e-book)

Library of Congress Control Number: 2022938073

For information about custom editions, special sales,
and premium purchases, please contact
specialsales@unionsquareandco.com.

Printed in China

2 4 6 8 10 9 7 5 3 1
unionsquareandco.com

Text by Courtney Gorter
Design by Gina Bonanno

CONTENTS

Dating can be difficult. No one's stumbling upon their soulmate right out of the gate; we all have to battle it out in the trenches of bad first dates and inexplicably canceled plans before we can even *think* about settling down with the one person we'll be sharing our french fries with for eternity.

And since no one knows the ins and outs of love in all its star-crossed glory quite like characters from the classics, who better to serve as your guide? The hopeless romantic in a Shakespeare play. The charming heroine in a Jane Austen novel. The ill-fated dreamer in pretty much anything by F. Scott Fitzgerald. These characters all walked that road before you, and they had to do it while juggling feuding families, the rigid constraints of nineteenth-century society, and the empty decadence of the Jazz Age. Given that the main obstacle standing between you and your crush is the fact that you just spent several hours crafting the perfect text only to receive a tepid "haha" in response two days later, it's fair to say you've got it easy! We can work with that! Or at least . . . our storied experts can.

Within these pages is everything you'll ever need to know about romance and relationships—from flirting to the honeymoon phase, from rocky roads to domestic bliss—courtesy of all the classic characters we know and love (and some we love to hate).

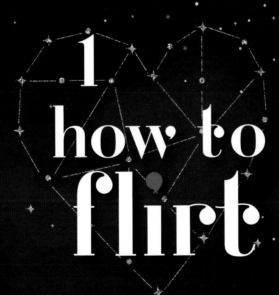

1
how to
flirt

W hat is flirting? At its most basic, flirting is just having a conversation with someone you wouldn't mind making out with and indicating, over the course of that conversation, that you wouldn't mind making out with them. Easy enough in theory, but surprisingly difficult to implement. If your idea of successful flirting begins and ends with saying hi to someone who not only hears you but also says hi back, well, you might just need some help with this. But don't worry! With the right advice, you'll be flirting, going on dates, and sussing out long-term compatibility over a plate of mozzarella sticks before the day is done.

HOW TO GO ON A DATE, ACCORDING TO JAY GATSBY

Nowadays there are many places from which to get advice, including the internet, Magic 8 Balls, and your mom. But if you're looking for dating advice specifically, then why not ask an actual expert in the field? Hi, I'm Jay Gatsby! And I'm going to get you a girlfriend the only way I know how: with perseverance, extravagant wealth, and blind optimism.

So there's this girl. I like her, but we can't be together. What should I do?

JG: I'm going to assume you guys can't be together because you're but a poor soldier of humble origins and she's a wealthy Southern belle with a pretty face and no sense of personal accountability.

Obviously.

JG: Right. So I'd start with proving your worth by acquiring lots of money through unscrupulous means. Girls like that.

Okay. So what's next? How do I ask her out?

JG: Whoa there. Let's slow it down. Let's take it easy there, buddy. You're lucky I'm an expert on this sort of thing. Do you think girls like a guy who shows *initiative*? Of course they don't! Girls like a guy who'll hook up with them, fade into obscurity for a couple years— maybe five—and only briefly resurface at some point to taunt them with cryptic love letters the day before they marry another man! This is basic stuff!

And *then* I ask her out, right?

JG: We're at least forty-three steps away from actually asking her out. I feel like you're just not getting this.

Sorry.

JG: It's okay.

So flirting? Is that what happens next?

JG: In a manner of speaking. What you're going to want to do is buy the mansion directly across the bay from hers and then throw a couple of parties for her benefit, all without ever actually inviting her or even speaking to her. Just stare at her house from time to time. Like, really eyeball it. As for the parties themselves, I'm talking big. I'm talking extravagant. I'm talking people getting run over in the driveway and guys fighting hobos in your garden. *Real* parties.

What if she doesn't live near a bay?
JG: Then I can't help you. God, you're making this difficult. Anyway, cultivate a widespread reputation so she'll hear talk of your riches long before the two of you actually reunite. You want your expensive cufflinks to speak for themselves. I think this courtship is going well so far. How do you think it's going?

I'm not sure. In this hypothetical courtship of ours, I haven't seen her in five years and also she's married to another man.
JG: Perfect! We've got her right where we want her. Now, coordinate a secret meeting between the two of you using as many mutual friends as you can muster, just to make things needlessly complicated. Don't forget to throw your shirts everywhere and almost fall down the stairs. This will be very sexy.

Okay, so we're reunited. That took a while. Are the two of us finally alone together?
JG: Certainly not, old sport! Your neighbor is there.

Why is he there?
JG: He helped you set this whole thing up. It'd be rude to ask him to leave, don't you think?

Speaking of leaving, is she going to leave her husband at any point? Maybe I could get her to run away with me?
JG: Yeah, she's not going to do either of those things. You guys *will*, however, embark on a secret, illicit affair. Her husband's suspicions will culminate in a loud, heated argument during which he accuses you of being a criminal and she ultimately chooses him over you. Your entire world will come crashing down around you and all you'll be able to do is watch.

That sounds terrible.
JG: It will be. I mean, not as terrible as when she runs over an innocent bystander while driving your car, but it's up there.

She runs someone over with my car?

JG: Yep. You're so in love with her that you even take the fall for it. Bet you wish you could go back to writing cryptic love letters and fighting garden hobos, huh?

I feel like I know even less about dating than I did before.

JG: Yes, well, I never claimed to be an expert.

That's exactly what you claimed.

JG: You've got me there.

So at the end of all this, I don't get the girl, and I wind up taking the blame for a crime I didn't commit. Could things get any worse?

JG: I don't see how.

9 CUTE DATE IDEAS

So you've finally done it. You've made a genuine connection with another person—you've established a mutual interest, you've followed each other on Instagram, and you've accidentally liked each other's selfies from 2013. What comes next is the tricky part: going on an actual date.

The reason this is so tricky is because every idea you'll have is just rife with potential disaster. Dinner and a movie? The movie could be terrible. A hike? Too sweaty. Apple-picking? Be serious. What if a bird swoops down and takes all the apples, and then there's a tornado?

If you're feeling stuck, you can't go wrong with these tried-and-true cute date ideas from classic novels and plays.

THE PHANTOM OF THE OPERA

Spirit her away to your lair beneath the opera house. Show her the underground lake. Play a bit of organ music. Nothing says "romance" quite like a hostage situation.

HAMLET
Try to get a little culture in your lives. See a play together—one that mirrors the events of your father's murder and will hopefully prove, once and for all, that your traitorous uncle was responsible.

MADAME BOVARY
Meet up at a cathedral. Hop in a cab together and spend the day driving around the city of Paris with the curtains drawn.

EMMA
Go on a picnic! Flirt with a man who's secretly engaged! Insult a kindly, middle-aged spinster! Get reprimanded by the family friend you'll one day marry!

1984
Meet in the room above Mr. Charrington's shop, striking out against the Party in one last hollow act of rebellion before your inevitable doom.

PRIDE AND PREJUDICE
Give her a tour of the grounds on your sprawling estate, forcing her to reevaluate her feelings, confront her own flaws, and envision herself as the mistress of Pemberley.

THE CATCHER IN THE RYE
Complain about all the phonies at your prep school, then abruptly ask her to run away with you with no planning or forethought whatsoever. To really sweeten the deal, be sure to angrily berate her when she points out the impracticality of this plan.

LES MISÉRABLES
Invite him to join a political uprising in Paris so the two of you will die together. Confess your love for him with your last dying breath and give him a letter from his girlfriend so he won't be mad at you in the afterlife.

THE PICTURE OF DORIAN GRAY→
Paint a portrait of him over the course of several sittings. Hopefully it won't come to reflect the evidence of his corrupted soul.

25 AUSTENIAN SIGNS SOMEONE HAS A CRUSH ON YOU

According to magazines, there are many ways to gauge the interest level of potential suitors (e.g., they touch their face a lot, their pupils get smaller, they straight-up say "I'm interested"), but nothing will ever be quite as valuable as the gems of romantic wisdom Jane Austen was dishing out all the way back in the early 1800s. Here is how you know, with absolute certainty, that someone has a crush on you:

1. They propose to you abruptly, despite the fact that the two of you can't stand each other.

2. They randomly show up at your estate with their relatives and appear ashamed for having behaved so poorly.

3. They carry you home after you sustain a twisted ankle. Later, they procure a lock of your hair.

4. They appear to have little interest in your modest inheritance.

5. They tell you right to your face that your spirited personality and your family's humiliating lack of propriety would make you an unsuitable bride for most men.

6. They accompany you to your family home and accuse your father of murdering your mother with no proof other than the fact that they've read a lot of Gothic novels.

7. They dance with you no more than is reasonable, lest this hideous breach of conduct cast an unsavory pall over your character.

8. They rebuff your advances on the word of an esteemed family friend yet pine for you for the next several years.

9. They discreetly pay off your sister's kidnapper.

10. They use their family connections to get your brother promoted from midshipman to lieutenant.

11. They leave town in the middle of your burgeoning courtship and refuse to answer your letters for many months.

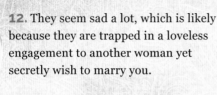

12. They seem sad a lot, which is likely because they are trapped in a loveless engagement to another woman yet secretly wish to marry you.

13. They purchase a horse for you in spite of the strain such an indulgence would place on your family's finances.

14. Having previously spurned you, they appear to have a change of heart when you become suddenly gravely ill.

15. They scold you for your foolishness and poor conduct, and are impressed by your attempts to make amends.

16. They secure you a carriage and offer you an umbrella should the weather prove stormy.

17. Though not much of a reader, they listen to you talk about your favorite books and promise to read whichever titles you suggest.

18. They urge you to write about them in your journal.

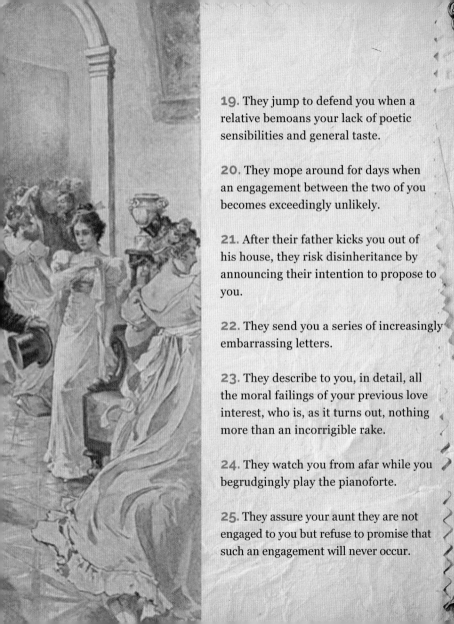

19. They jump to defend you when a relative bemoans your lack of poetic sensibilities and general taste.

20. They mope around for days when an engagement between the two of you becomes exceedingly unlikely.

21. After their father kicks you out of his house, they risk disinheritance by announcing their intention to propose to you.

22. They send you a series of increasingly embarrassing letters.

23. They describe to you, in detail, all the moral failings of your previous love interest, who is, as it turns out, nothing more than an incorrigible rake.

24. They watch you from afar while you begrudgingly play the pianoforte.

25. They assure your aunt they are not engaged to you but refuse to promise that such an engagement will never occur.

LITERARY DATING PROFILES YOU SHOULD REALLY CONSIDER USING

Anyone who has ever used a dating app before has agonized over what to put in their bio. It needs to communicate that you are witty and brilliant and also a good listener who works out and has a dog. But that's a lot of things to convey in three hundred characters or less! If you're stuck and really feeling the pressure, here are a few examples to get you started. (Disclaimer: only use these in your own bio if you want to get upward of a hundred matches *immediately*.)

JULIET CAPULET →

Just looking for something casual, and of course by casual I mean you would die for me.

DORIAN GRAY

I may be 38 but I've got the body of someone who traded his soul for eternal youth at age 20. (Not that I did that. I'm just saying.)

PENELOPE

I'll swipe right on someone just as soon as I finish weaving this funeral shroud for my father-in-law.

JAVERT

I know you're out there, Valjean.

THE WIFE OF BATH

Just a salacious storyteller and ale aficionado looking for her sixth husband. And if you're wondering what I like to do for fun, well, let's just say I have a gap between my two front teeth.

MRS. BENNET

Urgently seeking wealthy husbands of each of my five daughters. I've included pictures and ranked each one from most to least marriageable.

EDMOND DANTÈS

Not interested in anything casual. Also not interested in anything serious. All I'm really interested in is revenge.

OEDIPUS REX →

Just swipe left if you're my mom. There. Prophecy avoided.

HERA

I'm only here so I can see if my husband's using this app to cheat on me.

MR. ROCHESTER

My first wife is dead (for real) (I promise) so I'm trying to get back out there. Dealbreakers include checking out my secret locked room on the third floor, and also asking, "Hey, why is there a secret locked room on the third floor?

AURELIANO SEGUNDO

Expanding my radius because let's just say the dating pool where I live is pretty shallow.

SHAKESPEARE QUOTES YOU CAN TOTALLY USE ON A FIRST DATE

irst dates can be awkward at best and catastrophic at worst. And the most difficult part of a first date? Knowing what to say. Thinking up words, then saying them coherently . . . and in the correct order to boot. It's mostly just small talk, sure, but it's small talk with *stakes*. Screw this up and you've condemned yourself to a lifetime of making meals for one and enduring the relentless "So, still single, huh?" question at family parties.

There's a reason people call William Shakespeare the Bard of Avon—it's because the guy had a way with words (and was from Avon). Hidden among all the sonnets and soliloquies are perfectly worded responses to every conceivable first-date contingency. So the next time you're at a loss for words, don't worry; the Bard's got your back. Here's everything that can possibly happen on a first date, and what to say when it does.

What to say when you're late to the restaurant:

"O, forgive me my sins!"

—*The Tempest*, Act 3, Scene 2

What to say when you immediately spill something on the shirt you spent three hours picking out:

"Out, damned spot! out, I say!"

—*Macbeth*, Act 5, Scene 1

What to say when they introduce you to their parents over FaceTime at the restaurant:

"You have displaced the mirth, broke the good meeting, With most admired disorder."

—*Macbeth*, Act 3, Scene 4

What to say when your date blurts out "I love you" before the server has even brought out appetizers:
"Wisely and slow; they stumble that run fast."

—*Romeo and Juliet*, Act 2, Scene 3

What to say when the server finally asks if you're ready to order:
"I almost die for food; and let me have it."

—*As You Like It, Act 2, Scene 7*

What to say when they ask if you're going to eat all that and if you always eat this much:
"I am not bound to please thee with my answers."

—*The Merchant of Venice*, Act 4, Scene 1

What to say when your date is shocked you haven't heard of their favorite podcast so they begin playing the first episode right there at the table for you:
"Hell is empty and all the devils are here."

—*The Tempest*, Act 1, Scene 2

What to say when they start eating your onion rings without asking:
"Thou art a robber, a law-breaker, a villain: yield thee, thief."

—*Cymbeline*, Act 4, Scene 2

What to say when your date is clearly flirting with the server:
"If this were played upon a stage now, I could condemn it as an improbable fiction."

—*Twelfth Night*, Act 3, Scene 4

What to say when they have the gall to ask how much money you make:

"'Tis neither here nor there."

—*Othello*, Act 4, Scene 3 ↓

What to say when they ask you why your last relationship ended:

"Oh, that way madness lies; let me shun that."

—*King Lear*, Act 3, Scene 4

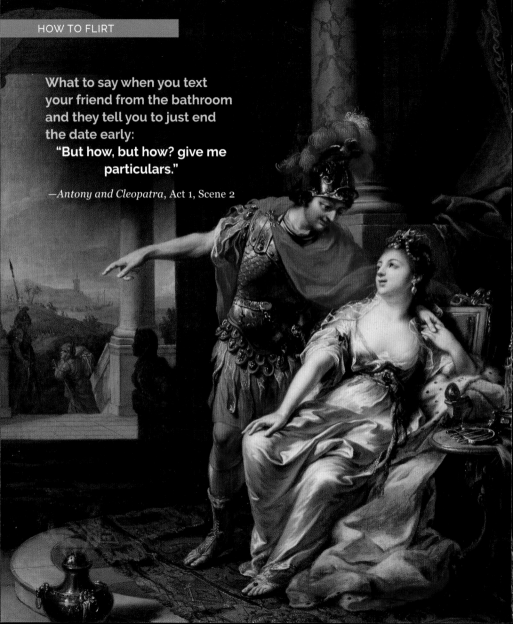

What to say when you text
your friend from the bathroom
and they tell you to just end
the date early:
   "But how, but how? give me
         particulars."

—*Antony and Cleopatra*, Act 1, Scene 2

What to say when you decide to proceed with the date anyway because you already bought tickets to the movie you guys were going to see afterward:
"Thus bad begins and worse remains behind."

—*Hamlet*, Act 3, Scene 4

What to say when the movie starts and the couple sitting in front of you won't stop talking:
"A plague o' both your houses!"

—*Romeo and Juliet*, Act 3, Scene 1

What to say when your date's phone suddenly goes off:
"Alack, what noise is this?"

—*Hamlet*, Act 4, Scene 5

What to say when they begin to have a conversation at full volume on their phone right there in the middle of the theater:
"Silence! one word more shall make me chide thee, if not hate thee."

—*The Tempest*, Act 1, Scene 2

What to say when the movie ends and you're standing idly outside trying to make your escape:
"Give me now leave to leave thee."

—*Twelfth Night*, Act 2, Scene 4

What to say when their ex shows up, begs them for a second chance, and then tries to fight you in the movie theater parking lot:
"This is too much."

—*Henry VIII*, Act 5, Scene 3

What to say when they're not taking the hint and ask if you're free this weekend:

"I am so full of businesses, I cannot answer thee acutely."

—*All's Well That Ends Well*, Act 1, Scene 1

What to say when he goes in for a good-bye kiss and you have to downgrade the situation to a farewell fist bump:

"Give me thy hand; 'tis late: farewell; good night."

—*Romeo and Juliet*, Act 3, Scene 3 ↑

What to say when they ask if you want to attend their cousin's wedding next month and you just have to come out with it:

> "Out of my sight! thou dost infect my eyes."

—*Richard III*, Act 1, Scene 2 ↘

What to say when they text you the next day asking for a do-over:

> "No!"

—*Hamlet*, Act 3, Scene 3

10 LITERARY FIGURES YOU'LL DATE AT SOME POINT IN YOUR LIFETIME

No one actually likes making small talk with a stranger over lukewarm coffee, hoping for the best (that they're normal and easy to talk to) but expecting the worst (they'll steal your wallet), but it's just something we all have to do so we can keep society going. So it stands to reason that you're going to date plenty of people in your life. Now, some of these people will be great and some of them will be terrible, and many of them will be one of the following figures straight of classic literature.

THE MR. COLLINS

The Mr. Collins is that guy who talks a lot (mostly about himself), or else he says, "Hey, does anyone want to know a fun fact?" and then the fact is far from fun. He rambles incoherently into the silence for a solid five minutes, holding you hostage with his long-winded dumbness. Eventually, you'll make a noise that could indicate "Wow, that's so interesting," but more than likely means "WHEN? WHEN WILL IT END? WHEN WILL DEATH COME?" at which point the Mr. Collins, thus validated, finally brings this meaningless TED Talk to a bumbling and anticlimactic conclusion.

THE PATROCLUS →

The Patroclus is that significant other who's always borrowing your clothes. Does he even have any hoodies of his own? He's been wearing yours for the past three weeks, so you're starting to wonder. It's very cute and all, this habit of his, and you're fine with it, obviously. But the fact remains that your favorite green sweater isn't where it usually is, and you really need it back. (Patroclus took Achilles's armor during the Trojan War, and look where that got him. Dead by Hector's hand is where.)

THE LADY MACBETH

The Lady Macbeth is the kind of partner who takes control whenever the situation calls for it. For instance, she'll cut off the "I don't know, what are *you* hungry for?" conversation at the knees and pick a restaurant without wavering. Simply put, she makes all the decisions and drives the relationship forward, wresting control of this

runaway train from the forces of chaos. People will call her things like "bossy" and "overbearing," but at the end of the day, did you or did you not decide on a Netflix movie to watch with minimal scrolling? Case closed.

THE LOGAN KILLICKS

This is the guy a family member set you up with. You gave it a shot and nobody can say you didn't, but the two of you have nothing in common. Sure, he's a homeowner (impressive!), but he wants you to do all the house and yard work and doesn't wash his feet before coming to bed. No thanks!

THE RAVEN

We've all dated this guy. He's always coming over unannounced in the middle of the night, he tends to stare blankly when you're visibly upset, he only ever gives you one-word responses—and that's to say nothing of his tendency to symbolize mournful, never-ending remembrance.

THE BEATRICE

The Beatrice is the one you would never, ever, ever date. Nope, not in a million years. Sure, she's charming and smart and witty and the two of you enjoy exchanging playful banter, and if pressed you might even admit she's the most beautiful woman you've ever met in your life. But you're totally not interested in her romantically. And if someone were to say she has a crush on you, you'd *barely* care, probably.

THE JOHN WILLOUGHBY

The John Willoughby will make you fall in love with him and ghost you with an intensity heretofore unseen, then come crawling back saying he misses you despite the fact that he's currently in a relationship with someone else.

THE TITA DE LA GARZA

Honestly? She's great. Her mom? Not so much. The Tita de la Garza is the love of your life—she's loving and compassionate, she can make one hell of a meal, and she kind of has magic powers. But she and her mom are a package deal, which means even if you were allowed to marry her, you'd be getting a fierce, unyielding, and manipulative mother-in-law in the bargain.

THE ODYSSEUS

The Odysseus is the partner you will date long-distance for so long that it feels like you've spent more time apart than together. Maybe he's studying abroad, or maybe the two of you go to separate colleges. Regardless, you will get extremely familiar with the ins and outs of Zoom dates. People will marvel at your willingness to date someone who's currently across the country ("I could *never* do that," they will say, eyes wide). And when you guys finally reunite, your relationship will be stronger for it, and he will slay the suitors in your feast room.

THE COUNT PARIS →

The Count Paris is that person your entire family wishes you would've ended up with. It doesn't matter how briefly you were involved, or even whether the totality of your relationship consisted of being engaged at your father's request and not much else—as far as your parents are concerned, the Count Paris in your life is The One Who Got Away. Even if nobody had died at the end of the play and Juliet had, in fact, ended up with Romeo, you can bet Lady Capulet would've taken every opportunity to say, "What's Count Paris up to these days? You two were great together. Do you guys still talk?"

2
the honeymoon phase

Y'ou've done it! You've navigated the labyrinthine journey known as casual dating and somehow emerged—elated and a little bewildered—on the other side, hand in hand with the person who chose you back.

So what comes next? Well, what comes next is the honeymoon phase. The honeymoon phase is basically the beginning of any love affair—that passionate, carefree period of time in the early days of a marriage or other relationship when everything is new and exciting—you're both floating hazily through life, secure in the knowledge that you're the first couple in history to experience this crazy, mixed-up thing called love.

HOW TO TELL IF YOU'RE IN THE HONEYMOON PHASE

No one *decides* to enter the honeymoon phase; one day you simply wake up and a cocktail of romantic neurochemicals is happening to you. Think you might be right smack in the middle of it? Here's how you know:

You can't get enough of each other. Sure, you just saw each other mere hours ago at the Capulet ball, but that doesn't mean you're not going to head straight to her house afterward and hope she's soliloquizing about how much she wants you, preferably on a balcony.

You're not sleeping much. Even the Friar has noticed, and he suspects you might have sinned with fair Rosaline.

You're in a perpetually good mood. So good that you refuse to engage in the tawdry squabbles of a blood feud that goes back generations.

Your partner can do no wrong. Either you're blind to his faults, or said faults simply don't bother you. You can forgive him for anything and everything, including slaying your dear cousin Tybalt in the town square and then fleeing the scene.

You feel everything much more deeply. Your emotions have been dialed up to eleven. At the slightest inconvenience, you will throw yourself on the ground and threaten suicide until someone has a better idea.

You can't stop talking about them. If Friar Laurence never has to hear you describe her blushing cheeks, soft hands, and sweet lips again, it will be too soon.

You want to spend all your time together. Even when one of you has been exiled to Mantua and will soon be hunted by the prince's men.

You always agree with each other. For instance, if you two spend one last night together and you point out that you need to leave because it's morning, and she says, "Okay but what about this: no it's not," you're probably going to say, "Good point."

You want it to go on forever. Does the honeymoon phase have to end? Usually. While it can last as long as two years, the honeymoon phase usually ends after several months. Yet, if you play your cards right—that is to say, if your relationship lasts all of a few days and results in the deaths of multiple people, including yourselves—the honeymoon phase can be your entire relationship. Violent delights have violent ends, after all.

WHAT THAT BOOK GIFT
REALLY MEANS

W'hen you're buying flowers for someone, it's important to remember that a rose means "I love you," whereas a ghost orchid means "I think you are unusual, expensive, and thrive in the swamplands of southwest Florida."

It's the same with books. When you're giving someone a book, your choice of book says volumes. And while it might seem romantic and thoughtful to give your partner a novel as a present (especially when the two of you first begin dating, eager as you are to portray yourself as Someone Who Has Read a Book or Two in Their Time), you need to understand what message you're sending with said book. For instance, if you give them one of the following, they're probably hearing this:

Love in the Time of Cholera—I have decided that I am going to marry someone else. Try me again in another fifty years.

The Epic of Gilgamesh—You are completely out of control, and I'm going to fight you.

Pride and Prejudice—I would date you in spite of your shortcomings.

Jane Eyre—You are not good-looking and everyone is constantly talking about it.

One Hundred Years of Solitude—It's difficult to differentiate between love and lust, and we're all doomed to repeat the mistakes of our ancestors.

The Old Man and the Sea—No pressure, but you're racing against the ever-tightening noose of time, and in all likelihood you will never accomplish anything.

The Great Gatsby—Our relationship is most likely going to end in either disillusionment or death.

The Picture of Dorian Gray—You are beautiful, selfish, and emotionally unavailable.

Catch-22—You are confusing and irrational, a problem that can't be solved.

One Thousand and One Nights—I'm planning on killing you eventually. We both know this.

Great Expectations—You will probably amount to very little without the help of a wealthy beneficiary who owes you a life debt.

Lord of the Flies—Given half a chance, I would not hesitate to cast off the shackles of polite society.

A Raisin in the Sun—I recently lost most of our money in a poorly planned investment.

The Metamorphosis—You've recently changed in a way that's inconvenient to me personally.

Their Eyes Were Watching God—The key to finding peace is becoming single and reflecting wistfully on lessons learned from past lovers.

↑**The Odyssey**—If we were separated for twenty years I would never take another lover, give or take a sea witch.

Moby-Dick—Depending on who you ask, you represent God, the devil, fate, mankind's quest for meaning, or the self-destructive nature of revenge.

Wuthering Heights—You have terrible taste in men and will probably die for it.

Of Mice and Men—I would definitely murder you if things got dicey.

Dream of the Red Chamber—The end of the feudal system was inevitable.

The Tale of Genji—I wish you were more like my mother.

The Importance of Being Earnest—You're absurd. Also, I do admire your silk cravat.

The Scarlet Letter—Do you mind if we keep our relationship a secret? Thanks.

Like Water for Chocolate—I hope we both die in a fireball, consumed by our passions.

Crime and Punishment—I know what you did.

11 LITERARY CHARACTERS SHARE THE MOMENT THEY KNEW THEY'D FOUND THE ONE

So you've been together for a while, and things are going great. Amazing, actually. But how do you know if this relationship has what it takes to go the distance? How do you know whether you've found *the one*? The moment is different for everyone, and since "I just knew" and "Something just clicked one day" are nonspecific and deeply unhelpful, we asked several literary characters to expand on the moment they knew they'd found their partner for life (however long that winds up being).

"From the moment I saw her across that crowded room, I knew I wanted to marry her and forget all about her cousin Rosaline, with whom I was in love not ten seconds previously."

—Romeo Montague on Juliet Capulet, *Romeo and Juliet*

"He was the first man I ever saw who wasn't my father or Caliban, so."

—Miranda on Ferdinand, *The Tempest*

"I knew he was the one for me when my dear cousin Algernon mentioned he had a friend called Ernest. There's just something in the name Ernest that inspires absolute confidence."

—Gwendolen Fairfax on Ernest "Jack" Worthing, *The Importance of Being Earnest*

"I knew I wanted to marry her as soon as I had the idea to poison my brother, thus clearing the way for me to become king of Denmark."

—Claudius on Gertrude, *Hamlet*

"I just feel like I've always loved her. Ever since I decided I needed a lady, or else what would be the point of all these acts of chivalry? She's totally real, though. Ask anyone. Gorgeous, too."

—Don Quixote on Dulcinea del Toboso, *Don Quixote*

"He was a living, breathing man on the wife hunt and I was a twenty-seven-year-old spinster. That's it. That's the whole story. What do you want from me?"

—Charlotte Lucas on Mr. Collins, *Pride and Prejudice*

"I saw her a couple times at the Luxembourg Garden and she didn't make much of an impression. Then one day I realized she was hot and that we were destined to be together. I then spent the next year thinking her name was Ursula. I guess you could say it was a storybook romance."

—Marius Pontmercy on Cosette Fauchelevent, *Les Misérables*

"I knew from the moment I saw a picture of her. Then she called me ugly while I was nursing her back to health and the rest, as they say, is history."

— Celie on Shug Avery, *The Color Purple*

"I'm the queen of the fairies, he's a mechanical with the head of a donkey. Needless to say, sometimes it just feels right."

—Titania on Nick Bottom, *A Midsummer Night's Dream*

"The first time we ever met, she was so mean to me I had to run away and cry for a few minutes. Of course, I immediately thought to myself, *Yep, she's the one*."

—Pip Pirrip on Estella Havisham, *Great Expectations*

"When I flirted with her and she wasn't having it, I just knew I had to make her fall in love with me if it was the last thing I did. What was the question again?"

—Henry Crawford on Fanny Price, *Mansfield Park*

QUIZ: Is He in Love with You, or Is He Just Obsessed with Recreating the Past?

Relationships are complicated. Sometimes you'll be totally in love with a guy and you'll think he's in love with you too, but it turns out he's simply yearning for something he can't get back. Take this quiz and find out if the passion between you is real or if he's just projecting expectations onto the idealized version of you he's created in his head.

1. When did he first tell you he loves you?
   a) One year into the relationship.
   b) After we went on our first date but before he ran off
      to earn a massive fortune.

2. Does he discuss his fears and insecurities with you?
   a) Yes, and we work through them together.
   b) Do you think a guy with a house that big (and with so many
      nice shirts to boot!) has *fears and insecurities?*

3. Has he introduced you to his friends and family?
   a) Yes.
   b) He only has one friend but I'm not even sure how close they are because he
      doesn't seem to know his real name (calls him "old sport" almost exclusively).
      Anyway I already knew that guy; he's my cousin.

4. Does he talk about future plans and goals with you?
   a) Yes, and he seems genuinely excited about the prospect of
      building a life together.
   b) Yes, and they all involve me leaving my husband.

5. What do you typically argue about?
   a) Money, communication issues, and division of household chores.
   b) Mostly we argue about the fact that I have a husband, and when
      exactly I'm going to leave my husband, and whether or not I ever
      actually loved my husband.

6. Before you guys started dating, how did he flirt with you?
   a) Love letters and poetry.
   b) He bought the house across the lake from me and just sort of pined in my general direction.

7. How does he show affection?
   a) Gift giving, compliments, that sort of thing.
   b) Generally by placing me on a pedestal and developing an obsession he'll then proceed to cultivate for the next five years.

If you answered mostly *A*s, he's genuinely in love with you!
There's no need to worry! He really does love you and isn't just drawn to the glamor, wealth, and status you happen to symbolize. We can't guarantee you guys are going to live happily ever after, but we *can* pretty much guarantee neither of you will end up dead in the pool because of the futility of the American Dream. So that's good!

If you answered mostly *B*s, he's just obsessed with recreating the past.
Sorry to say, but it looks like he's not so much "in love with you" as he is "haunted by what can never be." While you may think things are going great, you should know they're actually not. It's time to sit down and ask yourself the big questions, namely, "Is he in love with me, or is he just in love with the *idea* of me?" and "Is this worth risking my marriage over?" and "Of course it is, my husband's a jerk and a racist, why did I even marry him in the first place?" and "Why do I have such terrible taste in men?"

12 OUTFIT IDEAS FOR DATE NIGHT

If you're the type of person who always knows exactly what to wear, then you can just skip this one. Just leave the way you came.

For everyone else, can we all agree that picking out the perfect outfit for getting coffee is impossible? Especially when you've already been on a few dates, you're pretty sure they're your soul mate, the stakes are getting higher all the time, and they're picking you up in fifteen minutes.

Now, given that 90 percent of a date's success depends on the outfit you wear (that's a real statistic, but don't go Googling it or anything), it would behoove you to dress your best. Here are some stylish, easy-to-put-together outfits.

↑1. A pink suit. Like Jay Gatsby before you, you'll strike a dashing yet garish figure in a soft pink linen three-piece that just screams "new money." (This is especially sensible if the vibe you are currently giving off is "no money.")

←2. A tattered old wedding dress. Is this a little premature for a second or third date? Sure. But is it also bold? Absolutely. And since fortune favors the bold, show up to your movie date decked out in Miss Havisham's wedding dress, the lace yellowed from age, veil askew, one shoe on and one shoe off. And if your date stands you up, that's perfect! You already look like a jilted lover!

3. A red hunting hat. Some people are of the opinion that hats shouldn't be worn indoors, and especially not at the table. "This isn't a hat," you will say during your dinner date. "This is a symbol for Holden Caulfield's vulnerability, his need for isolation juxtaposed against his yearning for companionship."

4. A ham costume made from papier mâché and chicken wire. You'll be turning heads with this tasteful ensemble worn by Scout Finch in *To Kill a Mockingbird.*↗

5. A black velvet gown with a Venetian lace trim. Not unlike Anna Karenina, you'll command attention in this low-cut number paired with a wreath of pansies and a white lace sash. It's the perfect outfit for a fancy dinner date downtown, or possibly bowling. ⌐

6. A jester outfit. If it's good enough for Fortunato in "The Cask of Amontillado," it's good enough for you. Complete with fitted, multicolored fabric and a conical hat with jingly bells, you're sure to make a lasting impression. Just don't go following anyone into the catacombs on the promise of a fine vintage!

7. A dark, blood-splattered robe and mask. For a chic and put-together look, you can't go wrong with this wardrobe essential, favored by the mysterious party guest in "Masque of the Red Death" and symbolic of ever-looming doom.

8. Just all black. Gertrude may have told Hamlet to "cast [his] nighted colour off," but black is a timeless fashion staple. It's flattering, it works for every season, and it conveys to everyone present that you're not yet done mourning the death of your father.

9. An iron breastplate with chainmail. In addition to being both functional and fashionable, this will serve you well in the battle to come against Grendel's mother.

10. Animal skins. Trade your kingly clothing for animal skins to mourn your lost friend Enkidu. Forget the date. Set off in search of the Land of Night and the Waters of Death to seek immortality.

11. A scarlet letter A emblazoned on your gown for all to see. Originally intended as a badge of dishonor, this fun accessory marks you as an adulterer but will eventually come to represent your strength and evolving identity as you rise up above the constraints of Puritanical society. Plus, you can wear it with just about anything!

←**12. A white dress with puffed sleeves.** Pair it with a wide, floppy hat, and boom! Just like that, you're the spitting image of Maxim de Winter's first wife, Rebecca, whom he may or may not have murdered!

LITERARY VALENTINE'S DAY CARDS

I t's your first Valentine's Day as a couple, so it's probably in your best interest to go all out. We're talking flowers, chocolates, and an extremely specific Valentine's Day card that may or may not apply to your relationship but definitely applied to those of the following literary characters at some point or another.

Do you believe in love at first sight, or should I leave for five years and return a wealthy man, having acquired a vast fortune through bootlegging?

—*Jay Gatsby*

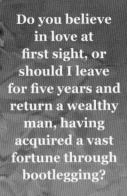

You're tolerable, but not handsome enough to tempt me.

—*Mr. Darcy*

I'm watching you, Valentine.

—*Big Brother*

Roses are red,
Violets are blue,
Elizabeth rejected me,
so I guess you'll do.

—*Mr. Collins*

I'm crazy for you, and also possibly just plain crazy.

—*Hamlet*

Okay, yes,
I murdered your
father and brother,
but only because
of how gorgeous
you are.

—*Richard III*

Whale you
be my
Valentine and
join me on a
monomaniacal
mission that
will almost
certainly end
in death?

—*Captain Ahab*

You can always
Count on me,
Valentine.

—*Dracula*

You're like a siren song—
beautiful, impossible to
resist, likely to lure me to a
watery grave.

—*Odysseus*

Not that I loved Caesar less,
but that I loved you more.

—*Brutus*

I love you,
~~Rosaline~~ Juliet.

—*Romeo Montague*

Don't be alarmed if this
card gradually begins
looking worse and worse.

—*Dorian Gray*

I'd love you even if
you were born—or
at least bred—in a
handbag.

—*Cecily Cardew*

Bye.

—*Remedios the Beauty*

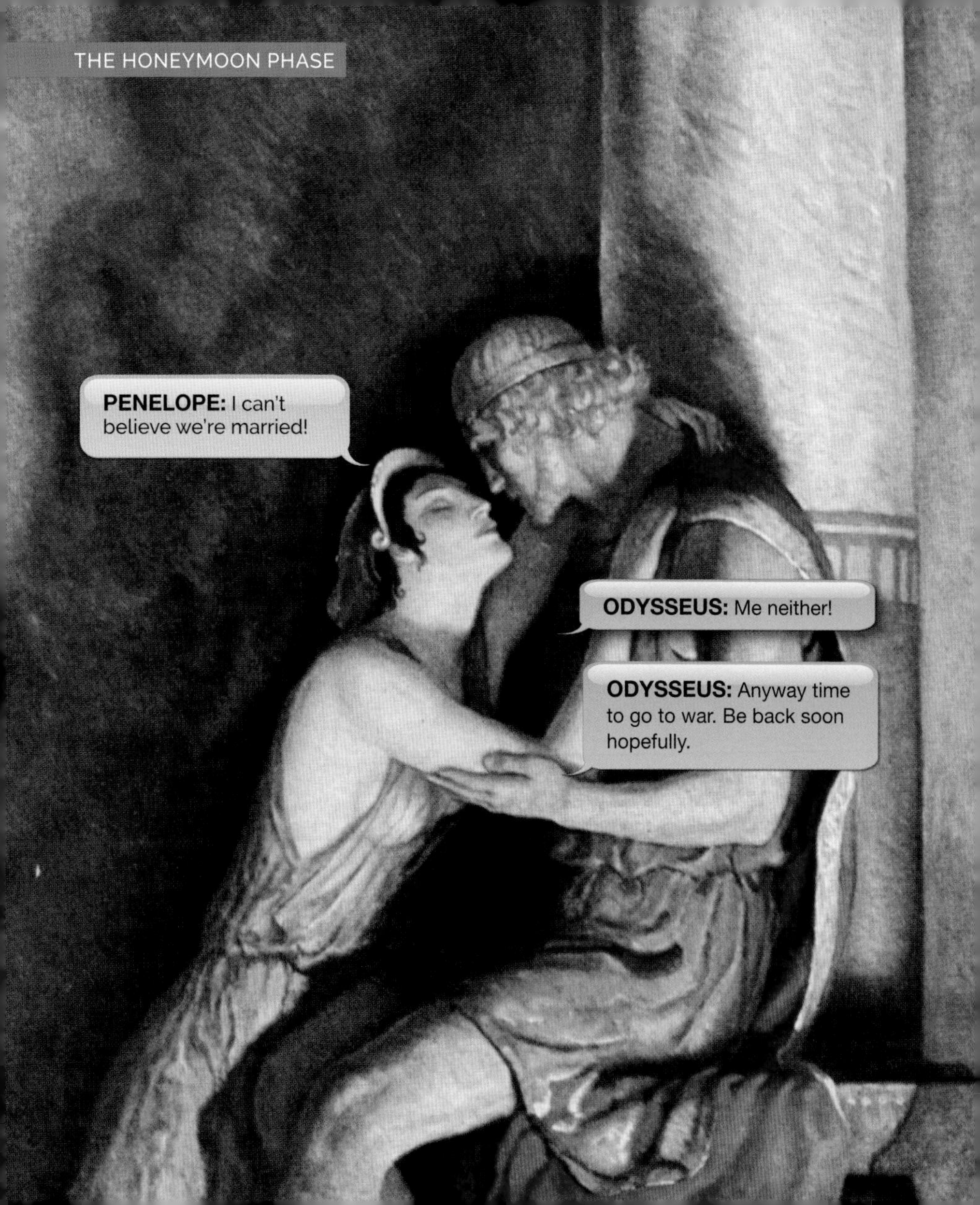
PENELOPE: I can't believe we're married!
ODYSSEUS: Me neither!
ODYSSEUS: Anyway time to go to war. Be back soon hopefully.

3
rocky road

No couple is perfect, and many encounter a rough patch at one point or another. Sometimes it's a trial to be worked through, and other times it's a sign to exit the relationship posthaste. Simply put, relationships aren't always smooth sailing. Eventually, you're bound to hit some rocky roads. Now that we've sufficiently mixed our metaphors, let's discuss relationships that are struggling, or just straight-up doomed.

17 Relationship Red Flags You Shouldn't Ignore

There are many things in life that are tempting to simply ignore (student loan payments, a text from your ex, that weird noise your car keeps making), but perhaps none quite as easy as red flags in an otherwise decent relationship. "I'm not seeing that," we tell ourselves at the first sign of trouble. "No, thanks," we insist when the red flags begin piling up.

Now, it's not always appropriate to randomly take off running, shrieking as you go, but that's exactly how you should handle the following red flags from literature should they ever make an appearance in your relationship.

ANNA KARENINA

A nearby stranger gets hit by a train the first time you meet. It's probably just a coincidence, but who's to say it won't foreshadow your horrific and untimely end?

THE EPIC OF GILGAMESH

All of her exes just so happen to meet terrible fates—the big ones are "is currently trapped in the Underworld" and "got turned into some kind of animal."

GREAT EXPECTATIONS

Her adoptive mother can be frequently heard muttering things like "Break their hearts my pride and hope, break their hearts and have no mercy!"

LIKE WATER FOR CHOCOLATE

He's not allowed to marry you due to a family tradition, so he marries your sister instead.

THE PHANTOM OF THE OPERA

He leads you to believe that he's an angel sent by your dead father.

A DOLL'S HOUSE

He refers to you as his "wife and child."

FRANKENSTEIN

He says he has a terrible secret but he can't tell you what it is until after you're already married, and if you happen to see him lurking around the property armed with pistols and daggers on your wedding night, mind your business.

OEDIPUS REX

You left home to escape a prophecy about killing your dad and marrying your mom, and the woman whose hand in marriage you just earned just so happens to be around the same age your mom would likely be. Also you killed a sort of dad-like man on the crossroads last night, but that's probably unrelated.

JANE EYRE

You frequently hear demonic laughing coming from the room you're not allowed to enter, and the housekeeper keeps trying to attribute the noise to one of the servants.

CRIME AND PUNISHMENT

He's really into Napoleon Bonaparte, and he has a secret.

←THE ODYSSEY

She lures you to her island with her irresistible song.

HAMLET

He puts on an antic disposition and bids you, "Get thee to a nunnery!" He later stabs your dad.

JOURNEY TO THE WEST

You're beginning to suspect the beautiful maidens seducing you are actually demons hoping to feast on your flesh.

THEIR EYES WERE WATCHING GOD

He gets bit by a rabid dog and then bites you.

A RAISIN IN THE SUN

He's good-looking and well-off but seems to have a problem with a woman having "thoughts."

ONE HUNDRED YEARS OF SOLITUDE

You both live in Macondo, and either don't know much about your family or haven't discussed it.

AGAMEMNON ⌐

She encourages you to walk on the purple tapestries despite knowing it's a sign of excessive pride and will almost certainly incur the wrath of the gods.

A Day in the Life of a Byronic Hero Who's Yearning for His Lost Love

W'hat is a Byronic hero? Named after Romantic poet Lord Byron (famously "mad, bad, and dangerous to know"), the Byronic hero is a world-weary, brooding type. He has a dark and mysterious past and loves to suffer, and his romantic life is often in total shambles. Literature is just full of these guys. Think Victor Frankenstein.

Think Heathcliff. Think Mr. Rochester. Now, given their moody misadventures and distressing dispositions, do you think their days look anything in the least bit like ours? Do you think any of them have time for banalities like "making lunch" or "getting the mail" or "folding laundry"? Please. Here's what they're doing instead.

6:45 a.m. — You awaken, though you slept in fits and starts. The weather is disagreeable. This is perfect.

7:00 a.m. — You don't eat breakfast. Breakfast is for contented people, and the French. Instead you use this time to languish moodily in your solitude and revel in being misunderstood. This takes at least an hour and a half.

8:30 a.m. — You gaze at a portrait of your beloved, sighing frequently. You usually lock the door to the Portrait Room, but today you forget, leaving it ajar. Hopefully a gentle and curious ingenue doesn't happen across it somehow and become consumed by the prospect of fixing you.

10:30 a.m. — You sulk.

11:00 a.m. — You lament.

12:00 p.m. — You suffer in silence. This involves quite a bit of sighing.

12:45 p.m. — You ready the horses and head into town.

1:00 p.m. — You wonder if today's the day you'll meet someone who isn't put off by your propensity to be an insufferable bummer. Might they find your aloofness . . . *charming*? Doubtful. Besides, you're not ready to love again. Not after what happened . . .

3:00 p.m. — People stare openly. They whisper as you pass. You sigh about it.

3:15 p.m. — You take care of several mysterious affairs.

4:30 p.m. — You reflect on your dark and troubled past, staring pensively out a window while a potential love interest looks on. She is intrigued by your sadness. Though she is of modest means, she has no designs upon your fortune.

5:45 p.m. — You attend a public event you do not wish to go to, arriving with a sweeping black cloak and a brooding disposition. You lurk in the background, casting a churlish eye upon the festivities. People watch from afar and liken you to a demon or vampire.

6:00 p.m. — You contemplate your rich inner life while occasionally muttering something akin to "What is the POINT of it all?"

7:15 p.m. — You embark on a brisk promenade through the woods, where you can be alone with whatever haunts you.

9:30 p.m. — Up until this point you've been acting mildly sullen and periodically whiny. Now it's time to roll up your sleeves and *really* wallow in your melancholy.

10:10 p.m. — You retire to your foreboding manor—sullen, lovelorn, and generally inconsolable.

10:45 p.m. — You think you see the ghost of your lost love, but it was merely a trick of the moonlight.

11:15 p.m. — You go to bed. You will lie awake for hours, until the nightmares claim you.

3:00 a.m. — You realize no ingenues wandered into your Portrait Room today. You are disappointed; the prospect of demanding they leave at once and slamming the door behind them seemed appealing. Perhaps tomorrow? You sigh.

HOW TO BREAK UP WITH SOMEONE, ACCORDING TO HAMLET

Breakups are never easy, but they're especially difficult when you're the Prince of Denmark and you're putting on an antic disposition to suss out erstwhile murder plots.

Now, I'm not saying I handled things perfectly, but I certainly handled them, eventually, and no one can say I didn't. Here's what to do when something's rotten in the state of your relationship.

I need to end my relationship. I still care about her, but we just want different things. I'm hoping to be gentle but firm. How should I do it?

H: Have you tried acting utterly deranged?

I'll be honest, I hadn't considered that.

H: It's not the *best* way to break up with someone, because when she tries to return your love letters and various other mementos you'll have to pretend you never sent her any, and that's obviously just a whole to-do.

I can imagine.

H: Maybe try asking questioning her honor and integrity in front of her dad.

Do I have any other options?

H: Making a bunch of sexual innuendos in front of her dad?

Does her dad have to be there?

H: Odds are that he's going to be eavesdropping nearby anyway, so it's best to just assume he'll be involved.

Is there any way I can end the relationship *without* calling her honor and integrity into question or making a bunch of sex jokes?

H: Not that I'm aware of.

Can't I just say I'm no longer in love with her?

H: Sure, you can say that. But you'll have to follow it up with the fact that you never loved her at all, actually, and that she should get herself to a nunnery stat, and then you should cap it off by cursing the very institution of marriage. And it wouldn't hurt to mention you hate women.

Are you saying *you* hate women? Like all women?

H: Yes.

Even your mom?

H: Especially my mom.

Okay, let's move past the "how" of all this and focus on the "where" for a second. *Where* exactly should I break up with her? My place? Her place? A park? Starbucks?

H: A random hallway will do just fine. Make sure she runs into you while you're contemplating the moral implications of suicide and the ways in which the unknowable void of death—that undiscovered country from which no traveler returns—makes cowards of us all.

I'll be sure to do that.

H: Because if you think about it, dying's a lot like taking a nap, but forever.

Are you okay?

H: No! Did I answer all your questions?

I don't think you answered any of my questions.

H: I disagree. I feel like we covered a lot of ground here. What else could you possibly need to know?

Ultimately, I'm hoping she and I can stay friends, but do you think we should take some time apart first?

H: Definitely not. In fact, if you want to attend a play and sit to her not long after, feel free to do so. You'll need to harass her with sexually explicit wordplay while simultaneously proving that your uncle murdered your father to steal the throne, after all.

What?

H: Although I wouldn't count on the two of you ever being friends again, especially after you stab her dad.

I wasn't planning on stabbing her dad.

H: Look, nobody *plans* on stabbing their ex-girlfriend's dad through a tapestry, but the fact remains that people hiding behind tapestries are notoriously easy to stab.

Who were you *trying* to stab?

H: My uncle, who's also my stepfather. Any other questions?

Just the one. Whatever happened to your ex? The one I assume we've been talking about this whole time?

H: After I stabbed her dad, you mean? She went mad. Just absolute crazy town.

What?

H: And then she drowned.

What?

H: I just got back from her funeral, actually. Now I'm on my way to fight her brother.

Good luck with that, I guess.

H: Thanks. And good luck with the breakup. Don't forget the sexual innuendos!

QUIZ: ARE THEY CHEATING ON YOU, OR HAVE YOU MERELY BEEN DUPED BY YOUR VILLAINOUS ENSIGN?

Are you having doubts about your partner's fidelity because someone with ulterior motives recently suggested that your boo might be cheating on you? Take this quiz to find out for sure.

1. Have they cheated in the past?

   a) Yes.
   b) No.

2. Are there large periods of time in their day that are
   unaccounted for?
   a) Yes.
   b) No.

3. Have you wronged anyone in your life? Someone who might
   take it upon themselves to set you up, for instance?
   a) Not that I know of.
   b) Just the guy I passed over for a promotion at work. Coincidentally this
      is the same guy who initially planted the idea that my partner might
      be cheating on me with the person I actually promoted, but other than
      that? No one comes to mind.

4. Do you have insecurities this person could possibly exploit?
   a) Not really.
   b) Not unless you're counting the fact that everyone says my partner
      doesn't actually love me and sometimes I wonder if they're right.

5. Do they have a friend who's in love with your partner and
   would surely agree to conspire against you?
   a) This is getting really specific.
   b) You mean Roderigo?

6. **Does your partner hide their messages from you? Do they take calls in the other room?**
   a) Constantly.
   b) No, but ask me about the handkerchief I gave her.

7. **Do they ever accuse *you* of cheating?**
   a) Yes.
   b) No.

8. **In general, has their behavior toward you changed at all?**
   a) They seem distant at times.
   b) No, they seem as in love with me as ever, that liar.

9. **Is there any actual proof?**
   a) Some, but nothing concrete.
   b) So much. You wouldn't believe how much proof. Iago said Cassio was talking about it in his sleep. And did I mention the handkerchief?

If you answered mostly *A*s, they might be cheating on you. (They also might not.)

We can't say for sure one way or another, but the fact that you're even taking this quiz means it's definitely time to sit down and have a conversation. It sure beats taking drastic action only to find out your standard-bearer had orchestrated the whole thing for his own nefarious purposes!

If you answered mostly *B*s, they're definitely not cheating on you.

It looks like your disloyal ensign did indeed stage an elaborate plot to make you doubt your partner's fidelity, either because you failed to promote him to the rank of lieutenant, or because he thinks you slept with his wife, or because he just felt like it. Thank God you took this quiz and didn't immediately give in to the classic Shakespearean rage response of "My beloved might be cheating on me? TIME TO LOSE IT."

9 CHARACTERS SHARE THE MOST DYSFUNCTIONAL RELATIONSHIPS THEY'VE SEEN

You know how we all have that friend who is dating someone terrible? And once every so often the two of them break up "for good," and you're like "Well, it's probably for the best; he *did* steal your television and burn down an orphanage," but one week later they're back together? That's almost exactly what it was like for the following characters to watch these disastrous love stories play out from the sidelines. You see, some literary romances give us an ideal to aspire to—a reason to keep trudging through the depressing swampland of bad dates and unanswered texts in the hopes that our very own happy ending is right around the corner. Unfortunately, these are not those romances.

"They toyed with one another's emotions and married other people, and when Catherine died Heathcliff decided the logical next step would be lock both their kids in the basement until they agreed to marry each other. Whenever someone says they want a love like theirs, I lose another year off my life."

—Nelly Dean on Heathcliff and Catherine Earnshaw, *Wuthering Heights*

←"He made her fall in love with a man who had the head of a donkey because she wouldn't fork over the kid she got from someone else. I know I helped, but the whole time I was thinking, *Oof.*"

—Puck on Oberon and Titania, *A Midsummer Night's Dream*

"You know, my dad once said never to judge people. Which I thought about doing, briefly, but then I watched a bunch of obscenely wealthy people cheat on each other all summer and the whole thing ended with three deaths. So I'm judging a little bit."

—Nick Carraway on Jay Gatsby and Daisy Buchanan, *The Great Gatsby*

"He called her chastity into question in front of everybody, drove her to fake her death, then agreed to marry a relative of ours as an act of penance. Let's just say I haven't decided against eating his heart in the marketplace."

—Beatrice on Claudio and Hero, *Much Ado About Nothing*

←"It doesn't get much more dysfunctional than killing your husband's new wife with a poisoned dress and then killing your own kids just to bring it all home."

—Aegeus on Medea and Jason, *Medea*

"Janie wanted romance; instead, she got twenty years of Jody, a man who only wanted a trophy wife he could control and belittle. No wonder she was all 'What a bummer. So anyway . . .' when he died."

—Pheoby Watson on Janie Crawford and Joe Starks, *Their Eyes Were Watching God*

"One time when I was attending the opera a chandelier fell from the ceiling and killed the woman I was sitting next to, all because the guy who lived in the basement wanted to watch his crush perform the lead role from a box seat."

—An opera patron on Christine and the Phantom, *The Phantom of the Opera*

"Imagine a governess agreeing to marry her employer, and when they break up it's not because he's old enough to be her father or because he pretended he was planning on marrying a richer, more beautiful woman just to make her jealous—no, it was because he was already married, and hiding his first wife in the attic! And then the governess wound up marrying him anyway! I mean!"

—Mrs. Fairfax on Jane Eyre and Mr. Rochester, *Jane Eyre*

25 WAYS TO TELL IF YOU ARE DATING A PLOT DEVICE

Dating can be pretty dicey. Some-times your significant other turns out to be a jerk, or a maniac, or a plot mechanism specifically devised to move the story forward. Now, those first two things are pretty easy to identify, but the third? Not so much. Don't worry. We know exactly how to tell when you're dating a plot device, and now so will you.

1. They don't seem to have a personality, a rich inner life, or any friends of their own, but they sure are making your primary love interest jealous.

2. The two of you are exchanging meaningful glances, but the very concept of love is forbidden under the current regime. You know you shouldn't. And yet . . .

3. They explain things. A lot of things. In fact, they seem to have a wealth of knowledge about many things, and they tend to pop up whenever things are unclear.

4. Conversely, they don't actually know anything. They pose all the questions you hadn't thought to ask.

5. Their untimely death (yikes! Sorry about that) ultimately spurs you into further action.

6. They often say things that later take on a strange significance.

7. You're perfectly content in your relationship when suddenly you spot them—a ruggedly handsome stranger in a public setting.

8. Your parents approve of them, and the two of you would make a good match, but you want to marry for love, not financial security!

9. They are your second romantic interest. Not your first, obviously. That's over. Well, it's mostly over.

10. Your relationship with them kickstarts a chain of events with dire consequences.

11. They are the exact opposite of your other love interest—almost like they exist to highlight certain qualities of theirs by contrast.

12. They experience little to no character development over the course of your relationship.

13. They are the boring, safe alternative to the person you'll actually wind up marrying.

14. They are constantly causing conflict in your social circle.

15. You were living one day to the next as a boring husk of a human being until they found you and gave your life new meaning, only to disappear shortly thereafter.

16. They're charming. Almost . . . too charming.

17. They're a really good listener, especially when you're monologuing.

18. The events of their life parallel a larger, more comprehensive theme.

19. They have a specific interest that comes in handy at a critical juncture.

20. You're beginning to suspect they represent something larger than themselves.

21. Their name is metaphorically resonant and chock full of hidden meaning.

22. They have an ironclad sense of right and wrong that will likely lead to their doom.

23. Villainous types are always using them to get to you.

24. They have a past they are strangely reluctant to talk about, but don't worry—it's about to become incredibly relevant.

25. They were the one that got away. But now they're back, and things will be different—you'll see.

4
domestic
bliss

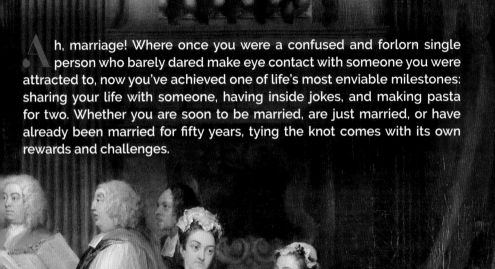

Ah, marriage! Where once you were a confused and forlorn single person who barely dared make eye contact with someone you were attracted to, now you've achieved one of life's most enviable milestones: sharing your life with someone, having inside jokes, and making pasta for two. Whether you are soon to be married, are just married, or have already been married for fifty years, tying the knot comes with its own rewards and challenges.

Mr. Darcy's Do's and Don'ts for Proposing

There's no wrong way to propose, except there totally is. Here's what to do—as well as what *not* to do, which can sometimes be just as valuable. Maybe even more valuable. (Don't do what I did, okay? Don't make my mistakes.)

DO tell her you ardently admire and love her.
DON'T follow this up with a long speech about how embarrassing her family is.

DO make sure you get the timing right.
DON'T do it immediately after she realizes your interference has ruined, perhaps forever, the happiness of a most beloved sister.

DO spend the majority of your proposal, you know, proposing.
DON'T speak at length about her social rank, and how it's vastly inferior to yours, and the fact that you're marrying her against your better judgment.

DO take her feelings into consideration.
DON'T assume she'll say yes just because you make ten thousand a year.

DO discuss the idea of marriage beforehand.
DON'T spend several months staring at her after making possibly the worst first impression of all time and then randomly blurt out a disastrous proposal one day in her best friend's home.

DO say things like "I can't imagine my life without you."
DON'T say things like "Could you expect me to rejoice in the inferiority of your connections?"

DO send her a letter afterward, conceding some of her points and correcting others.
DON'T rush things. Give it time; you both need to take a step back and reassess your behavior.

DO invite her to meet your sister at your impressive Derbyshire home.
DON'T let her status-seeking romantic rival criticize her appearance; make it known that your soon-to-be-wife is one of the handsomest women you know.

DO pay a morally bankrupt militiaman to marry her younger sister, thereby saving the entire family from ruin.
DON'T tell anyone. You're a changed man, after all. You don't need credit. She'll figure it out eventually anyway.

DO convince your best friend to marry her other sister and apologize for lying to keep them apart.
DON'T give up hope. She's likely refusing to let your aunt bully her into rejecting a proposal you haven't even made yet, which means there's still a chance!

DO propose for a second time, now without pride, prejudice, or any combination of the two. Tell her if she says no, you'll never bother her again.
DON'T despair. She's going to say yes this time (roughly a thousand misunderstandings later). Now all you have to do is get her family on board and live happily ever after. (You'll have to spend more time than you'd like

with the insufferable clergyman who's married to her best friend and has the patronage of your aunt, but still. Worth it.)

9 DAILY HABITS THAT WILL MAKE YOUR MARRIAGE STRONGER

Marriage isn't all flowers and poetry and sweeping declarations of love. It takes a lot of time and effort to make marriage work, and if you want yours to be successful (or at the very least not boring), here are nine habits you should try to incorporate into your daily routine.

Encourage each other! Is your husband struggling to screw his courage to the sticking place? Is he having trouble deciding whether or not to kill the king of Scotland? Channel your inner Lady Macbeth and give him the boost he needs by pointing out that *real* men murder their kings without hesitation, and also that he's already promised to do it.

Reignite the spark! In *Sir Gawain and the Green Knight*, Lord and Lady Bertilak decide to spice things up by throwing a Knight of the Round Table into their marriage. Have *you* tried spicing things up by throwing a Knight of the Round Table into your marriage? ↓

Ask them how their day was! It's possible the answer will be "Well, not great so far. Our pet parrot escaped again, and also I found out my friend was a cannibal," but unless your husband is Dr. Juvenal Urbino from *Love in the Time of Cholera*, hopefully the chances of that happening are slim.

Surprise them! Don't let your marriage grow stale. Reunite with them after twenty years and shoot an arrow through a line of twelve axes.

Accept each other's differences! Like the fact that one of you is a Montague and one of you is a Capulet.

Check in with each other! "I'm still the town pariah in case you were wondering," Hester Prynne might text her husband in *The Scarlet Letter*. "Cool," Chillingworth might respond. "I'm a little busy psychologically torturing your secret boyfriend at the moment. Talk tomorrow?"

↑Talk about the future! Share your hopes, dreams, and plans for what's to come. And if a soothsayer has been telling your husband, "Beware the Ides of March," well, that's definitely a conversation you need to be having.

Take up a hobby together! For Monsieur and Madame Thénardier in *Les Misérables*, this involved scheming, mischief, and general villainy.

Give them space! Just ask Mr. Collins and Charlotte Lucas in *Pride and Prejudice*; sometimes the best thing you can do for your marriage is to leave your spouse alone for long stretches of time.

WEDDING ANNIVERSARY GIFT IDEAS

Paper for your first anniversary? Wood for the fifth? Tin for number ten? Get out of here! Whoever planted the inaccurate yet pernicious idea that *cotton* is an acceptable anniversary gift for having made it twice around the sun in holy matrimony is clearly wrong. For a marriage that's sure to stand the test of time, try these themes and ideas from classic literature instead.

FOR YOUR FIRST ANNIVERSARY, THE THEME IS *THE PICTURE OF DORIAN GRAY*.
This is typically the year you get your spouse something *The Picture of Dorian Gray*–related, such as a portrait in the attic that ages in their stead, growing hideous while they remain youthful.

FOR YOUR SECOND, THE THEME IS *SIR GAWAIN AND THE GREEN KNIGHT*.
To celebrate your second year as a married couple, give your partner a green girdle that may or may not protect them from being beheaded.

←FOR YOUR THIRD, THE THEME IS "*THE GIFT OF THE MAGI*."
Sell your hair to purchase a chain for their watch. Surely they won't in turn sell their watch to buy you combs.

FOR YOUR FOURTH, THE THEME IS *TO KILL A MOCKINGBIRD*.
Whittle them a doll made out of soap in their likeness. Stick it in a tree and hope they find it.

FOR YOUR FIFTH, THE THEME IS *THE THREE MUSKETEERS*.
A sword, a horse, and a letter to join the Musketeers will do nicely.

FOR YOUR SIXTH, THE THEME IS *DREAM OF THE RED CHAMBER*.
Send them two used handkerchiefs. This gift will confuse your maid, but certainly your lover will understand.

FOR YOUR SEVENTH, THE THEME IS *BEOWULF*.
Give them rings, an embossed helmet, a banner, and eight horses with gold bridles as thanks for defeating Grendel.

FOR YOUR EIGHTH, THE THEME IS *LIKE WATER FOR CHOCOLATE*.

Now's the perfect time to give them a box of matches that symbolizes the contents of their soul, compelling them to figure out what sparks their life's fire.

FOR YOUR NINTH, THE THEME IS *SENSE AND SENSIBILITY*.

Nine years together, and you still haven't given them a lock of your hair? Do you even love them at all?

FOR YOUR TENTH, THE THEME IS GREEK MYTHOLOGY.→

Like wily Odysseus in the tenth year of the Trojan War, you're sure to be praised for your creativity on this one. Simply construct a big wooden horse and leave it where they'll find it. They'll bring it within the walls of the impenetrable city of Troy, thereby ensuring a decisive victory for the Achaeans.

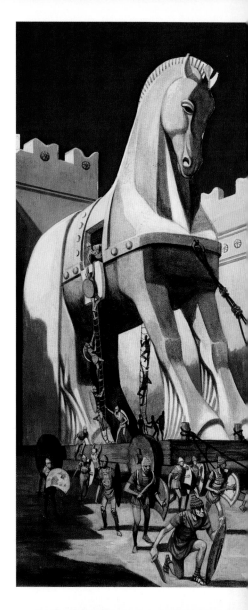

DEAR LADY MACBETH: AN ADVICE COLUMN

How do you know if you're ready for marriage? *Is* there a correct way to load the dishwasher? When you kill a man, does the blood on your hands ever truly wash off? We're here to answer those questions and more in "Dear Lady Macbeth," a weekly advice column about the ups and downs of all things marital.

Dear Lady Macbeth,

My husband is a huge flirt. He says it's harmless, but it's starting to affect our marriage. How do I get him to stop talking to other women?
—*Feeling Frustrated*

Dear Frustrated,

Well, that depends. Are these "other women" the witches three? Did he meet them in fog and filthy air? Are they chanting and cackling and predicting he'll be king thereafter? If that's the case, I say let it go. In fact, encourage a follow-up conversation. See what they know about Macduff.

Dear Lady Macbeth,

My husband is constantly inviting people over without asking me and expecting me to entertain multiple people for dinner with very little notice. How do I communicate to him that this doesn't work for me?
—*Perpetual Hostess*

Dear Perpetual Hostess,

Do you think I wanted to entertain King Duncan and his attendants at Inverness after the former Thane of Cawdor's execution with no time to prepare? Of course I didn't! But sometimes we all have to do things we don't want to do, including accommodating unwelcome houseguests. (It helps if you know the unwelcome houseguest in question won't live to see the sun rise. Just something to think about.)

Dear Lady Macbeth,

My spouse and I both have full-time jobs, yet I find myself doing 99 percent of the housework. How should I handle this?

—*Tired of Being the Only One Doing the Dishes*

Dear Tired,

Tell your spouse that marriage should be an equal partnership. One person makes dinner, the other does the dishes. One person walks the dog before work, the other after. One person murders the king of Scotland at the prompting of three bearded women in the woods, the other finishes the job and blames the servants when the first person panics.

Dear Lady Macbeth,

My husband is a flake. He often forgets important dates or promises to do things and then doesn't. How can I get him to take this stuff more seriously?

—*At the End of My Rope*

Dear End of My Rope

Real men honor their commitments. Explain this to him. If he requires further convincing, casually mention that you yourself would murder a baby if you'd previously sworn to do so. That should do the trick.

Dear Lady Macbeth,

My husband frequently embarrasses me in public. Should I say something to him, or just grow a thicker skin?

— *Embarrassed*

Dear Embarrassed,

My advice? Just be glad he's not shouting at an empty chair in the middle of a royal banquet while all the lords of the land look on. Now *that's* embarrassing.

Dear Lady Macbeth,
I think I've fallen out of love with my spouse. How do we get that spark back?

—*No Longer in Love*

Dear No Longer,
Contrary to popular belief, marriage isn't about love. I mean sure, it helps, but marriage is more about committing heinous acts in the name of steely ambition, berating your spouse because he's reluctant to murder a close personal friend, and dismissing his fears whenever he starts going on about things like "feeling guilty" and "getting caught." Want to get that spark back? Kill a man together, thus plunging the country of Scotland into total chaos.

Dear Lady Macbeth,
My wife makes more money than me, which makes me feel insecure and less than manly. What should I do?

—*Outmanned*

Dear Outmanned,
My advice is to leave your wife. That way she can find a new husband who isn't a coward.

Dear Lady Macbeth,
My husband and I got a divorce after I discovered his affair, but we still share a Netflix account. What should I do?

—*Cheated On*

Dear Cheated On,
Look the innocent flower, but be the serpent under it. (Wait until they release the latest season of his favorite show, then change the password.)

LAST-MINUTE RELATIONSHIP ADVICE FROM LITERARY CHARACTERS

Well, that's it! You now know everything there is to know about romance. "Wait, really?" I can practically hear you saying. "Everything?" Yes, everything! You know how *not* to ask someone out (if you're stealing them away to your subterranean opera house lair, you've done something wrong), you know how many people are likely to die as a result of your star-crossed affair (it's six), and you know the odds of your boyfriend having a secret wife in his attic are something like 40 percent. What else is there to know?

But before you close this book and dive back into the world of dating, armed with knowledge that will at best secure you a coffee date and at worst leave you dead in the pool because your girlfriend ran over her husband's mistress with your car, we'll leave you with a few more pearls of wisdom just to bring it all home.

"The last thing you want your proposal to be is 'thoughtful' or 'romantic' or even 'good.'"

—Mr. Collins, *Pride and Prejudice*

"Girls love it when you take the blame for their vehicular manslaughter."

—Jay Gatsby, *The Great Gatsby*

"If you're going to set a fire, start with the curtains. Those go up real quick."

—Bertha Mason, *Jane Eyre*

"Men only want one thing, and it's a series of interconnected bedtime stories with cliffhangers."

—Scheherazade,
One Thousand and One Nights

"The best advice I can give is to write your crush a love letter and immediately leave the room."

—Captain Frederick Wentworth,
Persuasion

"Marry your best friend, unless he's poor, in which case marry the neighbor."

—Catherine Earnshaw, *Wuthering Heights*

"Love is a choice you make every day, and so is never washing your feet before bed, *Logan*."

—Janie Crawford,
Their Eyes Were Watching God

"Dating is full of ups and downs, especially when you're an unmarried woman in the Regency era and your family's estate is entailed to a male heir."

—Elizabeth Bennet, *Pride and Prejudice*

"If there's one thing I've learned, it's that sometimes your uncle is hiding behind the tapestry, and other times it's just some guy. And that guy is your ex-girlfriend's dad."

—Prince Hamlet, *Hamlet*

"Look, jealousy happens. And your spirit leaving your body to attack your lover's other mistresses? Sometimes that also happens."

—The Rokujō Lady, *The Tale of Genji*

"Never choose a wealthy, arrogant guy who just wants a housewife over a charming, thoughtful guy who challenges you intellectually and offers to help you move."

—Beneatha Younger, *A Raisin in the Sun*

"Love conquers all."

—Dorothea Brooke, *Middlemarch*

"No it doesn't."

—Werther, *The Sorrows of Young Werther*

"When given the choice between a family member you've known your entire life and a man you met literally yesterday, choose the man you met yesterday. I can't believe I even need to say this."

—Juliet Capulet, *Romeo and Juliet*

"So what if she marries someone else? Just wait fifty years. He's gotta die eventually. It's called playing the long game."

—Florentino Ariza,
Love in the Time of Cholera

"Marriage shouldn't start with a lie, but it's fine if the lie winds up being true."

—Jack "Ernest" Worthing,
The Importance of Being Earnest

"The best way to leave your terrible husband is curse him and run off with his lover, who is now your lover."

—Celie, *The Color Purple*

"If the man you love is in love with someone else, have you tried going to sleep and waking up in a forest? I find that usually does the trick."

—Helena, *A Midsummer Night's Dream*

"If you sleep with the maid, she *will* accuse your wife of witchcraft."

—John Proctor, *The Crucible*

"Just marry the richest, best-looking person who will agree to marry you back."

—John Willoughby, *Sense and Sensibility*

"Don't put your trust in the wrong people; you'll get arrested for a crime you didn't commit right before your wedding, and one of the guys who put you in jail will marry your bride."

—Edmond Dantès,
The Count of Monte Cristo

"You can never have too many husbands, and old men make for boring lovers but are very easy to blackmail. I hope this was helpful."

—The Wife of Bath, *The Canterbury Tales*

PICTURE CREDITS

Alamy: *Artepics: 23, 66, 99; History and Art Collection: 44; Masheter Movie Archive: 61; The Picture Art Collection: 16, 69; Science History Images: 105*

Art Resource, NY: *HIP: 36*

Courtesy of Artvee *4, 10, 13, 24, 26, 28, 32, 33, 47, 56 bottom, 64, 74, 76, 96 inset, 98, 101, 102 bottom, 110, 112, 121, 122 inset*

Birmingham Museum & Art Gallery: *18*

Bridgeman Images: *ii, 21, 29, 71, 91; ©A. Dagli Orti/©NPL–DeAPicture Library: 70; ©Blackburn Museums and Art Galleries: 14; ©Christie's Images: 80; ©Ferens Art Gallery: 43; Lebrecht Authors: 54; ©Look and Learn/Private Collection: back cover, 41, 60, 74, 83, 104; The Stapleton Collection: vi, 48, 51, 88*

Courtesy of Cleveland Museum of Art: *115*

Courtesy Everett Collection: *11, 52 bottom, 53 right, 55; ©Warner Bros. Pictures: 53 left*

Courtesy of Folger Shakespeare Library: *27, 31, 38, 40, 106, 107 top, 109, 116*

Getty Images: *CSA Images: 20;* DigitalVision Vectors: *clu: v; duncan1890: 39, 96, 102 top, 108;* E+: *lleerogers: 106;* iStock/Getty Images Plus: *DenPotiev: 30; geengraphy: throughout (lettering); L Feddes: 107 bottom; Nnehring: 109; OlgaLebedeva: i*

Courtesy of Metropolitan Museum of Art: *19, 94*

MUTI: *7 bottom, 81, 82*

Courtesy of Rijksmuseum: *6, 9, 68*

Shutterstock.com: *Sveta Aho: 6–9 (border); akilev: 38–40 (background); AlevtinaZ: 48–51 (border); Amovitania: 18–19 (background); Rodin Anton: 6–9 (background); Artchi art: 99 top center left; Artishok: 122; BigMouse: throughout (text bubbles); DigitalMagus: 14 (paper); ECOSY: 13 (heart); etry0: 96–98 (background); Extezy: 80–83 (background); gillmar: 41–43 (ribbon); glaz: 15; Infografx: 27; irina_angelic: 99 top left and right; ivangal: 20; jakkaje879: i; Khramtceva Mariya: throughout (constellation heart); Klaus Kunster: 102 (doodles); Larisa1: 70–73 (background); lavendertime: throughout (sky); LiliGraphie: 96 (frame), 107–109 (background); local_doctor: iv; Lyonstock: 120; Andy Magee: 80–83 (border), 96–98 (border); MagicPics: throughout (hearts and arrows); Milan Manojlovic: 39 (rose); Merydolla: 17 middle; mimomy: 103 middle; Mitoria: 100–101 (doodles); mmalkani: 76–79* *(border); Nadine.de.trevile: 103 right; Ozz Design: 57–59 (valentines); Galla Pilina: 52 top; P.S.Art-Design-Studio: 56 top; Irina Rakyta: 99 top center right; Polina Raulina: back cover (heart); boonchai sakunchonruedee: 88–90 (background); Natalia Sedyakina: 110–114 (background); Solar.Garia: 28, 44 (floral heart); Boris Sosnovyy: ii; Dan Thronberg: 103 left; Gorbash Varvara: 7 top, 8, 9 top; vectorimage: 76–79 (background); Courtesy of Smithsonian National Museum of American History: 97; Svetlana Vorotniak: 57–59 (ribbons); VVSV: 16 left; Yoko Design: spine, throughout (heart quill)*

Courtesy of Wikimedia Commons: *14, 75, 79, 86, 100; National Gallery of Victoria: 84*

Courtesy of Yale Center for British Art: *73*

ABOUT THE AUTHOR

Courtney Gorter is a copywriter and humorist. Having studied English literature at the University of Michigan, she is currently a content strategy manager at SparkNotes, and her work has appeared on McSweeney's and Romper.